ANIMALS AT RISK

Rhinos In Danger

BY LYDIA SNYDER

Gareth Stevens
Publishing

Please visit our website, www.garethstevens.com. For a free color catalog of all our high-quality books, call toll free 1-800-542-2595 or fax 1-877-542-2596.

Library of Congress Cataloging-in-Publication Data

Snyder, Lydia
Rhinos in danger / by Lydia Snyder
pg. cm. — (Animals at risk)
Includes index.
ISBN 978-1-4339-9160-8 (pbk)
ISBN 978-1-4339-9161-5 (6-Pack)
ISBN 978-1-4339-9159-2 (library binding)
1. Rhinoceros (Genus)—Juvenile literature. 2. Endangered species—Juvenile literature. I. Title.
QL737.U63 S67 2014
599.66'8—d23

First Edition

Published in 2014 by
Gareth Stevens Publishing
111 East 14th Street, Suite 349
New York, NY 10003

Copyright © 2014 Gareth Stevens Publishing

Designer: Andrea Davison-Bartolotta
Editor: Therese M. Shea

Photo credits: Cover, Cover, pp. 1, 5 (both) iStockphoto/Thinkstock; p. 6 f9photos/Shutterstock.com; p. 7 Steve Bloom/Taxi/Getty Images; p. 8 Kletr/Shutterstock.com; p. 9 Dennis Donohue/Shutterstock.com; p. 10 Ulga/Shutterstock.com; p. 11 javarman/Shutterstock.com; p. 13 Brooke Whatnall/Shutterstock.com; p. 14 Gelia/Shutterstock.com; p. 15 Jami Tarris/Workbook Stock/Getty Images; p. 17 Mary Plage/Oxford Scientific/Getty Images; p. 18 Mike Simons/Getty Images; pp. 19, 20 Mark Carwardine/Peter Arnold/Getty Images; p. 21 Mr. Timmi/Shutterstock.com.

Printed in the United States of America

CPSIA compliance information: Batch #CS13GS: For further information contact Gareth Stevens, New York, New York at 1-800-542-2595.

CONTENTS

Words in the glossary appear in **bold** type the first time they are used in the text.

ALL IN THE NAME

The name "rhinoceros" comes from two Greek words. One means "nose," and the other means "horn." This big creature's name says it all! Rhinoceroses, or rhinos, have either one or two horns above their nose. These horns continue to grow throughout a rhino's life.

There are five rhino **species**: Sumatran rhinos, Javan rhinos, black rhinos, white rhinos, and Indian rhinos. Sadly, all are in danger of becoming **extinct**. People are working to increase their numbers, but more needs to be done.

WILD FACTS
Rhino horns are made of the same matter as your fingernails and hair.

Javan rhinos and Indian rhinos have one horn.
Sumatran rhinos, black rhinos, and white rhinos have two.

Indian Rhino

White Rhino

5

Who are the rhinos' greatest enemies? People are! People have taken over rhino **habitats** to build homes and farms. That means rhinos have less land to find food. They have less chance of having a family, too.

Another effect of smaller habitats is that rhinos may leave **reserves** to look for more food. Rhinos can be deadly if they come across people. Though large, they're quite fast. They've been known to **charge**, killing whatever—or whomever—is in their way.

WILD FACTS

Birds sit on the back of rhinos and eat the bugs that land there.

Rhinos don't have good eyesight. This may be another reason they charge. They don't know if what they see is dangerous.

Poachers are people who hunt illegally. Poachers kill rhinos and sell their parts, especially their horns. In areas of Asia, ground-up rhino horn is thought to cure certain illnesses. Its effects have never been proven, however. Some people even think the horns are magical! Other parts of a rhino, such as its skin, are used for similar purposes.

Some poachers let the rhino live after taking its horns. However, rhinos need their horns to fight off enemies such as lions.

WILD FACTS
Rhinos may live up to 50 years.

Some people who want to **protect** rhinos remove their horns before poachers can kill the big animals. This is still harmful.

9

WHITE RHINOS

The white rhinoceros of Africa is the largest of all rhinos. It may stand more than 6 feet (1.8 m) tall at the shoulders, be 15 feet (4.6 m) long, and weigh 3.5 tons (3.2 mt)!

In southern Africa, the population of white rhinos in the wild has leapt from fewer than 100 animals in the early 1900s to more than 20,000 today. Years of protection have helped their population grow. Hopefully, similar laws and methods can help other kinds of rhinos.

WILD FACTS

Female white rhinos live in groups with their babies, called calves. Most adult male white rhinos live by themselves.

 White rhinos are no longer called **endangered**.
However, they're still "threatened."

BLACK RHINOS

Black rhinos also live in Africa. Both black rhinos and white rhinos are actually gray! You can tell them apart by their mouth. The black rhino has a pointy upper lip it uses to tear fruit and leaves off trees and shrubs. The white rhino has a square-shaped lip that's perfect for eating grass.

Also like white rhinos, black rhinos have two horns. The longer front horn is used for protection and to dig into the ground. Only about 4,800 black rhinos remain in Africa.

COMPARING BLACK AND WHITE RHINOS

BLACK RHINO
- pointy upper lip
- eats fruits, leaves
- endangered

BOTH
- two horns
- gray color
- live in Africa

WHITE RHINO
- square-shaped upper lip
- eats grass
- threatened

Rhinos like being dirty! Mud keeps bugs off their skin and keeps them from getting sunburned.

Asian rhinos have folded skin that looks a bit like **armor**. The Indian rhino is found in the northeastern part of India and Nepal. It's sometimes called the greater one-horned rhino because it has one horn and is the largest of the Asian rhinos.

Hunting and habitat loss reduced the Indian rhino population to about 600 by 1975. Some had been killed

just to keep them from eating crops. Laws were created to protect these rhinos. Today there are about 2,900 Indian rhinos.

In the 1800s, Europeans and Asians hunted rhinos for sport.

The Javan rhino has one horn. It looks a lot like the Indian rhino though a bit smaller. That's why it's sometimes called the lesser one-horned rhino.

Laws haven't helped all rhinoceroses. Though Javan rhinos once lived in many Asian countries, poachers and hunters did great harm to this species. There are fewer than 50 Javan rhinos left and these live in just one national park in Indonesia. There are so few that scientists have a hard time counting and tracking them.

WILD FACTS
Scientists have placed cameras with sensors on trees in order to count the Javan rhinos.

Javan rhinos are the most threatened of all the rhino species.

SUMATRAN RHINOS

Sumatran rhinos live in the mountain forests of a few Southeast Asian countries. As the smallest rhinos, Sumatran rhinos weigh about 1,760 pounds (800 kg) and grow to a height of about 5 feet (1.5 m) at the shoulders. They can be 10 feet (3 m) long.

Sumatran rhinos are the hairiest rhinos. They have reddish-brown skin, too. Sumatran rhinos have two horns, but the horns are much smaller than African rhinos' horns. These creatures, too, face extinction. There are fewer than 200 left today.

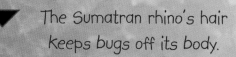

The Sumatran rhino's hair keeps bugs off its body.

19

CAUSE AND EFFECT

Some people think keeping rhinos in zoos will protect them. However, rhinos in **captivity** rarely have calves. This isn't the answer.

People must change their ways. If people didn't buy rhino horns, there would be fewer poachers. And if people allowed rhinos enough land on which to find food and have families, rhino populations would grow. People all over the world need to understand how their actions affect rhinos and other animals in danger.

RANGER ON RHINO RESERVE

Rhinos in the Wild Today

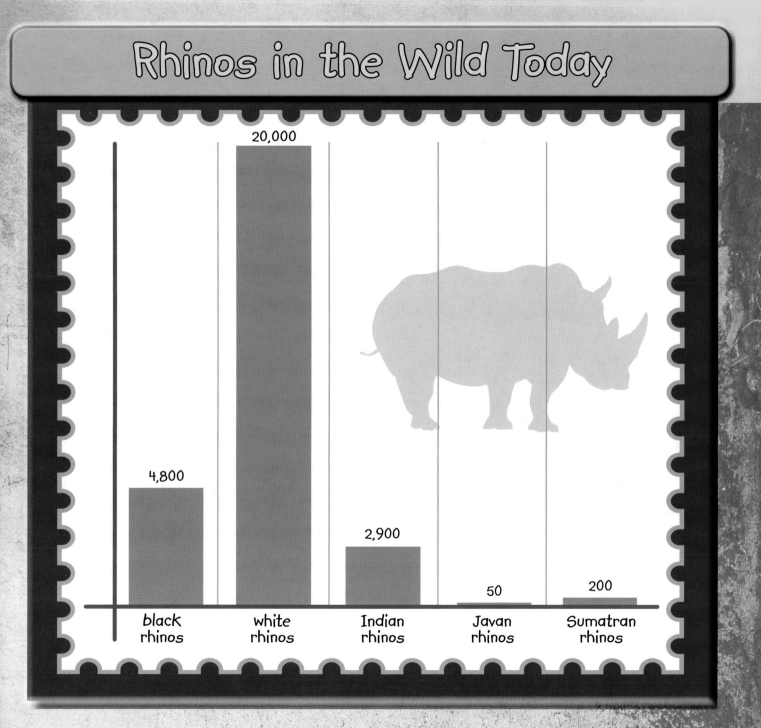

20,000

4,800

2,900

50

200

black
rhinos

white
rhinos

Indian
rhinos

Javan
rhinos

Sumatran
rhinos

GLOSSARY

armor: a thick covering worn to keep someone safe from harm

captivity: the state of being caged

charge: to attack by rushing forward

endangered: in danger of dying out

extinct: no longer living

habitat: the natural place where an animal or plant lives

protect: to guard

reserve: a safe area for endangered animals

sensor: a tool that can detect changes in its surroundings

species: a group of plants or animals that are all of the same kind

FOR MORE INFORMATION

BOOKS

Green, Jen. *Rhinoceros*. Danbury, CT: Grolier, 2009.

Orme, Helen. *Rhinos in Danger*. New York, NY: Bearport Publishing, 2007.

Suen, Anastasia. *A Rhinoceros Grows Up*. Minneapolis, MN: Picture Window Books, 2006.

WEBSITES

Mammals: Rhinoceros
www.sandiegozoo.org/animalbytes/t-rhinoceros.html
Read about all five species of rhinos on this zoo website.

Saving Rhinos
wwf.panda.org/what_we_do/endangered_species/rhinoceros/
Find out what is being done to save rhinos—including what you can do to help!

INDEX